What I Couldn't Say

Marissa Harding

Copyright © 2025 Marissa Harding
All rights reserved, including the right to reproduce this book
or portions thereof in any form whatsoever.
ISBN: 979-8-218-76450-0

Publisher: MH Press

DEDICATION

For those who made space for me,
for Ms. Labau and Mrs. Zanteson,
who saw the writer in me
before I knew she was there.
Thank you for your light.

PREFACE

I've spent the last two decades writing through joy, heartbreak, silence, and everything in between. These poems have lived with me across many versions of myself, each one carrying its own truth.

As I step into a new decade of life, it feels right to finally share what, until now, has lived mostly in notebooks and quiet spaces. This collection holds a wide range of experiences from trauma and healing to love, nature, self-reflection, and growth.

There is softness, and there is ache. I let both speak.

My hope is that within these pages, someone finds comfort, solace, empowerment, or inspiration. Whatever it is they may need.

These words helped me find my voice. If you're searching for yours, I hope they remind you it's there.

Part I – The Earth Speaks

Twilight

The twilight drips down my arms,
Like honey from the throat of the sky.
It stains the sea,
Turns every stone into a secret flame.

I walk inside its bruise,
And feel the stars begin to speak.
They call me to the silence
Where your hands once lived,
Their voices soft as bread,
Their tongues heavy with ash.

The wind unbuttons the horizon,
Night rises from the water's mouth.
I carry its weight in my chest,
A dark sweetness
That remembers your name.

Early Dawn

I awakened to the horizon,
Captured by the early dawn.
The lingering cold air tickles the spine,
Raindrops bouncing lightly upon the window pane.
The humming of sweet life,
A sonata resonating within eternity.
An artistic fog like a cloud permeates
A landscape once parched and dry.
A raw essence that instills us
With renewal of the soul.

Simplicities

Truth's simplicities entwined as one,
The sweetness of the moment beguiles any complexity.
Seasons begin to fuse every fabric of our being.
The darkness begets renewal.
Inspiration thrives, engulfing the vapor of despair.
Lips remaining famished,
A longing for enchantment,
A bittersweet salvation for my kindred soul.

Marissa Harding

The Hour That Asks Nothing

I have found joy
In the sparrow that drinks from a puddle,
In the bread that rises slow
On the hearth of ordinary hands.

The river does not hurry,
Yet it carries all things to the sea.
The pine does not shout its wisdom,
Yet its silence heals my ear.

The world asks little of us.
It is we who demand
Gold for our breath,
Crowns for our hunger.

But I have chosen
To lay my head upon the field,
To count wealth
In the cool hand of water,
In the single apple given,
In the hour that asks nothing
And gives me the sky.

Wind

The wind came through.
I listened. I wanted to understand what it said.
It had a voice, but not one I could keep.

Maybe it carried stories—
Of old wars on dry ground,
Of people crying because they had to,
Of journeys that ended too fast.

Maybe it still carries the dreams of people no one remembers.
Or maybe it only brings the smell of rain or fire or dust
And leaves it on our skin.

Did it pass a starving child before it touched my face?
Did it move through the sleeves of men waiting in the dark,
Their rifles cold and their hearts not much warmer?

It was cool when it reached me, damp.
It smelled like leaves that had given up.
The trees moved when it passed. They listened.

I think it wants to speak.
It hums at my windows and runs through the roof tiles.
I try to answer. I try to hum back.

But I don't know the tune.

Morning Hush

Touched by shades of gray, pellucid skies,
A gentle autumn rain to awaken morning's hush,
Branches reaching for the heavens,
As their hues continue to fall,

Tickling the earth,
A glint of sunshine upon ripened grains,
The crisp breeze waltzing the leaves,
Woven with the sweetness of autumn's breath.

The scent of pine begins to captivate,
A sequence that never sleeps.

Winter Waits

Beneath winter's splendor
Lies an earth awaiting
The whispers of merriment and wonder.

Other worlds remain dormant, longing for warmth.
The wind recites its ageless melody.
Village lights linger as the moon watches in silence.
Darkness lays siege upon the day.

Fall With Me

Fall with me before the crystal sea,
As daylight stirs pigments
That caress a lifetime.

Fall with me while we listen to the waiting bird,
The song of a timid heart,
A faintly heard splendor.

Fall with me into a silent night.
Breathe the sacred sighs,
Let the sky paint itself.

Fall with me upon the moon.
As motion slows, stars disappearing one by one,
Permeating beauty surrounds a world unknown.

The River

There was a river once.
It moved like a song you knew
Before you had words.

It ran cold in spring
And warm by August,
And the fish were always gone
Before you could see them.

We were young then,
Not in age, just in thinking
The world would wait.

The porch creaked in the dark.
You said something about the stars.
I didn't answer.
The air was too still,
And your voice had already gone
Somewhere I couldn't follow.

Later,
When the fields turned gold
And we drank from bottles
We didn't need,
I remembered the river.
I thought it might still sing.

But it doesn't.
It's quiet now.
Like you.
Like me.

Marissa Harding

The Bark Cracked At Dawn

The bark cracked at dawn,
A sound sharp as glass in the cold.
The tree held its silence,
But I heard the years inside it split.

It stood there patient and scarred,
Roots gripping the earth like truth.
The wound was not its ending,
Only the place the light could enter.

I thought of my own body then—
How time has pressed against my ribs,
How silence has bent my voice,
But still I rise to meet the morning air.

The tree and I,
Both marked by weather,
Both carrying our broken lines,
And still alive in the frost of day

On The Soul In Storm

The soul does not fear the storm,
For it was born of thunder
And carries lightning in its breast.

The body trembles,
Walls shudder,
The heart beats against its cage,
But the soul stands unmoved,
Like a cedar in high wind.

Do not curse the storm.
It comes to cleanse the air,
To strip the branches bare,
To teach the root its strength.

When the waters rise,
The soul rises with them.
When the wind breaks the doors,
The soul becomes the door.

The storm is not your enemy.
It is your inheritance.
It is the song of the earth,
Calling the spirit home.

Burning Season

The wind stole the last drink from the grass,
Its mouth full of fire.
Smoke curled into my lungs.
The drought had come again.

Rain last week meant nothing—
A drop in a dry bucket.
Elsewhere, skies opened.
They drank.
We waited,
And the fields turned to flame.

Hell had a face.
It watched me through the heat.
I ached for rain.

My tongue was ash,
My journal ash.
The words blew from me like sparks.

Still I lived.
Now I write in a shelter,
Borrowed ink, loaned paper.
This is the new chapter:
I write with smoke in my hair,
And with hope.

Wildfire Psalm

The ridges cough embers into the throat of night.
Pines lift their dark green prayers,
And the fire answers in gold.

Ash drifts down like slow snow,
A soft confession.
The stones glow with a hunger older than grief.

I put my hand to the ground.
Beneath the char,
A heartbeat still works,
Beating through smoke,
Refusing to be only what burns.

The Patience Of Stones

Stones keep the secrets of rivers,
Of hooves, of rain.
They speak without tongues
And endure without praise.

Lay your grief upon them,
And they will not break.
They teach the soul
To be a quiet mountain,
To bear the storm without becoming it,
To shine only when the sun remembers.

The Last Bee

A little engine of gold
Threads the clover alone.
The meadow waits in silence,
Its choir undone.

One hymn remains—
Thin as a wing,
Heavy as the world.

Sky Burden

Clouds drag their gray bellies across the sun.
The air tastes of iron,
A rumor of rain,
A rumor of ending.

They stoop lower and lower,
Pressing their silence into my chest.
I breathe, and the weight enters—
A storm waiting for its name.

The trees stand rigid,
Their leaves turned like coins of warning.
Birds stitch a frantic seam across the sky,
Then vanish into the dark seams of roof and branch.

Even the earth holds its breath,
Soil swollen, impatient,
Every blade of grass bristling
For what must come.

I lift my face, and the sky presses closer,
Its vast hunger folding into mine.
When the first drop falls,
It burns.

The Whisper Of Autumn

Clouds gather at the rim of day,
Calling their council before night descends.
A sudden tongue of lightning speaks,
And a frog leaps into the hymn of rain.

Summer lingers still,
Yet autumn waits behind her,
First as a whisper at the edge of the field,
Then in full glory,
Her breath gilding the leaves.

Beneath my window,
A single leaf hangs in a cobweb,
Its gold trembling in the cool wind.
An old man dreams nearby,
His thoughts turning like the seasons.

In the garden,
Chrysanthemums bow in their forgetting.
Brown comes to the earth.
The trees loosen their treasures to the wind,
And in the mingling of leaves,
Neighbors become kin.

Footsteps fall softly on a trail of pink petals,
Tracing the wind's path,
Swirling like noisy leaves,
A gust of sparrows.

Maidens In White Skirts

Snow gathers the shadows,
Pouring them into each footprint
Until the ground becomes
A map of blue pools.

The wind moves through the trees,
And the trees answer,
Their old bones speaking in creaks and sighs.

In this place without men,
I walk with one bird beside me,
And we share the silence.

Above the fountain,
Snow swirls in slow circles,
Maidens in white skirts,
Turning to greet the season.

They lift their hands,
And winter, generous and unhurried,
Fills them.

Without Proclamation

Spring came without herald, and I could not tell the day of her arrival,
Yet I had felt her presence early,
In the lengthening light and the tempered air that met me at my threshold.

She approached not as a stranger asking entrance,
But as the rightful occupant returning to her domain,
And the naked trees, long patient, received her in their quiet company.

In the first warm rains she laid her hand upon the soil,
And at once the earth, which had so long withheld its breath,
Opened to receive her.

The water ran in delicate threads between the roots of the birch,
And the air was filled with that ancient, subtle perfume
Which belongs neither wholly to the year past nor to the year to come.

Such rains, gentle and insinuating, prevail where the violent fail;
For they coax rather than compel,
And I reflected that the affections too are best awakened
By kindness and not by force.

Soon the days waxed in warmth,
And the red maple stood in its modest bravery before the orchard
ventured a bloom.
Presently the apple boughs whitened,
As if in secret converse with the sun concerning their appointed hour,
Each fulfilling its term without haste.

The hum of the bee sounded early in the noonday air,
And their ancient industry, untroubled by the gaze of man,
Appeared itself a kind of worship,
Whereby the blossoms were made the more steadfast in their labor.

Often in the night she came unperceived,
Moving with the moon's own stillness;
Yet in the morning there lay upon the grass
A brightness not of the day before,

And the breath of the meadow entered at my open window.

I awoke from dreams wherein green pastures and running streams
Mingled with a strange contentment,
And thought how natural it is for the mind to grow prolific
When the earth herself quickens to the season.

Thus, without proclamation, she took possession,
Converting the brown field to pasture,
The pasture to garden, and the garden to a richer scene still,
Until all wore the livery of her reign.

And walking among these changes,
I perceived it to be a law of Nature
That as she renews herself,
So too is man renewed if he will but stand still long enough
To be worked upon by her transforming hand.

Symphony Of Spring

Brilliant flashes cleave the dark,
And rouse the heavy rain.
Its silver feet on tin descend,
And sound their soft refrain.

A breath, and then the heavens break
With sudden iron will.
The windows shake, the china sings,
The startled cats grow still.

My own heart leaps to meet the sky,
And answers with its beat.
This year the spring proclaims her name
With power fierce and sweet.

The daffodils came long before
And would not turn away.
Their yellow crowns through frost endured
And keep their place today.

Now blooming trees and tangled shrubs,
And dandelions near,
Are met by storms whose symphonies
Remake the waking year.

Within that loud unbridled sound,
My winter soul takes wing.
For joy has found its root again
And blooms with early spring.

Blossom-Bound

The beauty of a day like this
Leans softly at my door.
Its breath is warm upon the field
Where winter dwelt before.

Blossoms rise from secret roots
As if they knew the way.
The meadow finds its emerald voice
And learns again to say.

The ice unclasps the quiet pond
And frees the mirrored sky.
Its loosened fingers brush my heart
And let the coldness fly.

A petal in the shadow wakes
And dares the tender air.
The hour holds me like a seed
That dreams what it will bear.

The birds begin, and all the trees
Are drawn into their song.
The earth turns over in her sleep
And wonders what is wrong.

But spring has come and set her hand
Upon the stirring ground,
And all who feel her gentle claim
Are blossom-bound.

Edge Of Day

I watch the silver water turn
Beneath a sky of mist.
The tide pulls secrets from the deep
The shore has never kissed.

Its breath is soft against the hull,
It rocks the boat in rhyme,
And whispers names the currents keep
From any tongue but time.

The foam is lace upon the waves
That fold and drift away
To meet the place where light and salt
Become the edge of day.

The Dance Of Swans

I gaze into the vast bluish grey expanse
Where each droplet of crystal light
Falls toward the sands of time
As if returning to a place it once called home.

In the small hands of an angel
These moments are held as though they might last forever.

Wings open to the breath of warm currents,
Carrying the soul northward
Past the silent music of stars and planets,
Through bands of light whose names we have never known.

Dreams travel with us
Until wandering thieves steal them into their own keeping.

Fingers weave stardust into the cloth of night.
Colors shimmer in red, green, gold, silver, and bronze,
Like promises unbroken.
Diamonds turn slowly in the air,
Seeking to adorn the dance of the swans
Who glide through the sky as if it were water.

Love Becomes The Light

Snow bends upon the cedar's arm,
And stars attend the sky.
The frost has etched the meadow's face
With scripts the winds supply.

A candle burns within the dark,
Its language warm and clear.
It speaks without the aid of speech
To any soul that's near.

No gift is sought from gilded hand,
Nor from the merchant's store,
But only that the heart be lit
And keep its winter door.

For when the holly turns to flame
Within the hush of night,
All sorrow folds into the pine,
And love becomes the light.

The Seed Chooses

The frost does not descend
To leave the meadow bare.
It breaks the clods and wakes the seeds
To seek the tender air.

Each wound becomes a door
To rooms you could not see.
The tide recedes, and on the sand
Lies what was meant to be.

The love that ebbed away,
The fire that burned too long,
Revealed the path you had not turned
And where you don't belong.

The end you thought was all
Taught branches how to bend.
The crack you feared would pull you through
Became the water's friend.

The storm is not a chain
But where the roots drink deep.
It is the hour the seed will choose
What blossom it will keep.

Red Rose

A touch beyond grotesque yet beauteous,
A loss that yearns for a kind heart.
As the rouge bleeds upon her petals,
'Tis among her stem
She reigns over love's domain.

With thoughts that do entice,
A fulfillment so thine and sweet,
Exalting the soul,
A vivacity beginning to wither.

An allure once opulent and heavenly,
No longer entwined with sublimity,
But a departed ode from reality,
Red rose.

Roots

Beneath the soil a quiet labor continues.
Roots drink the dark
And hold the hill to itself.

They do not hurry,
Counting wealth in rain and time.
What we call silence
Is work without witnesses.

Kneel, and press your ear to the ground.
You will hear the earth keeping its promise,
One patient thread at a time.

The Mountain Waits

The mountain waits.
It does not hurry.
Its silence is a breath
Drawn across centuries.

Snow lays its hand upon the summit,
Then slips into rivers below.
Clouds lean against its shoulder
And move on.
Still it remains.

I placed my hand on the granite,
And the stone gave nothing
But the knowledge of endurance—
A strength beyond speech,
An age beyond measure.

It has watched the hawk's circle,
The deer crossing at dusk,
The endless procession of stars.
Storms have broken upon it,
Yet morning always returns,
And the mountain does not bow.

I thought of my own brief hours,
My restless search for meaning,
The way I scatter myself
In questions without answers.

The mountain spoke only by standing.
And in its stillness
I found enough.

Part II – Love, Loss, And The Quiet Between

Closed Off

Closed off,
Walled in,
Not because I want to be,
But because pain taught me to stay hidden.

Fear of breaking,
Fear of being left,
Keeps the heart quiet,
Keeps the soul small.

Still, I reach,
Still, I long for arms that are not there,
For a voice that says,
You are not alone in this world.

Sunlight tries.
It pushes through the cracks.
It warms the cold corners
Where even memory forgot to live.

A hand finds mine.
Hope flickers.
Lips meet.
Lips part.
But something gentle stays behind:
A whisper,
A beginning.

You came with a softness I did not expect,
A steady voice,
A quiet strength.
You did not fix me.
You stood with me.
And that began the healing.

Not all angels fly.
Some speak in stillness.

Some love without asking.

And now,
The heart that once froze itself to survive
Has begun to feel,
To breathe,
To live.

Call It Mine

Don't talk to me
About fading.
I still feel.

Don't need fire in my hips
To know I'm burning.
These hands have held too much
To forget the weight of skin.

Don't call it memory.
I'm still here.

The world once came to me
Like a storm,
Hungry and loud.
Now it comes like a hum,
But it comes.

The mouth still waters.
The neck still arches.
Don't let the gray fool you.

I remember wanting
Like a second heartbeat.
And I still want.
Not the kind that begs,
But the kind that knows.
The kind that says,
Come here
If you know how to stay.

I've known the rush.
I've known the ruin.
Now I want the touch
That stays after.

The look that doesn't flinch

When the light hits the scars.

Age didn't take my hunger.
It made it sharper.
Made it honest.

I don't need soft words.
I need real ones.
I don't want fireworks.
I want the warmth
That stays lit
After the smoke clears.

Call it what you want—
Desire,
Longing,
Life.
I call it mine.

Have I Fallen

In pre-dawn light I watched you sleep
And wondered at my rest.
The calm you brought inside my chest
No longer called a guest.

Your touch has healed what once was raw
And filled the silent space.
I never knew that I could fall
And land in such a place.

Your eyes have met me to the core,
No glance has struck so deep.
And now your kiss, a quiet drink,
Has taught my heart to keep.

No joy like yours has reached my soul,
No smile that ever stays.
I touch your hair, I kiss your mouth,
And praise the giving days.

And when sleep comes to close my eyes,
I whisper, yes, I see.
The truth is written in my chest,
That I have fallen fully.

A Chance

A chance to hold you close at last,
To let the silence cease.
To fold the pain we carried long,
And open into peace.

You know how much you mean to me,
How much I'd give to see.
If dreams could step from sleep to day
And set your spirit free.

Though hope may seem too far to reach,
It lingers just the same.
It grows within the smallest seed
And answers to your name.

No other love could match our song,
No other voice could stay.
So let the dream become the truth,
And love not drift away.

He Is

He walks without hurry,
And the earth seems to part for him.
I believe it does.

His eyes hold light,
Not fierce,
But calm like water
When the sun speaks softly.

His words carry weight,
Not from volume,
But from truth.
They are stones shaped by the river,
Worn by knowing.

When I sit beside him,
Time forgets to press against me.

He laughs,
And the trees lean near,
Not out of need,
But wonder.

In his arms,
The world does not vanish—
It becomes gentle.

He gives without asking,
Loves without proving.
His presence is enough.

Once I searched for flame.
Now I know the warmth
Of a steady light.

I do not ask why he stays.
He is here.

And that is enough.

In his stillness,
I remember how to love.

I Wish Your Heart Were Like Your Words

I wish your heart were like your words,
So steady in their tone.
You speak of love, then turn away
And face the dark alone.

You talk as though the pain has passed
But hold it like a flame.
You cannot bear the cost of love
Yet long to feel its name.

You stand apart, untouched, unclaimed,
Your sorrow wrapped in pride.
Afraid to fall again too deep,
You choose instead to hide.

But love, when true, must risk the fall
And take the open hand.
The Lord still offers healing there
In ways you misunderstand.

So take a step, and lift your eyes,
And speak what longs to live.
To let the past be past at last
And learn again to give.

He Is Beautiful

He is beautiful, not just in face,
But in the way he stands.
A spirit sharp with thoughtful grace
And steady working hands.

His mind moves like a winter stream
Through thickets thick with snow.
Yet in his heart, a steady flame
Continues still to glow.

He speaks the truth and bears the storm
With wisdom worn and wise,
The kind you find once in your life,
Like stars in quiet skies.

He is the warmth I run toward,
The calm I cannot fake.
And when I rest within his arms,
My soul no longer aches.

Enough

I found a quiet blooming in you,
Not one that sought the sun,
But one that opened
Because it was time.

You did not strive to change,
And still you grew.
You stood as the pine does,
Unconcerned with being noticed,
Content in its place among the trees.

Your glance did not pierce,
But revealed.
It led me not to question,
But to remember something ancient
And still.

When the world trembled,
You did not resist it.
You bent,
And in that bending
You remained.

Your name became part of my breath,
Not spoken aloud,
But carried in the rhythm
Of ordinary hours.

You speak of your flaws
As if they lessen you,
But I have seen how light
Falls most beautifully
On the broken bark of trees.

You have given me no performance,
Only presence.

Not fire that devours,
But warmth that endures.

Even your shadow carries life.
Even the winding path
Has always led me home.

And if one day we walk apart,
And winter comes between our steps,
Know that my love
Will rest beneath the frost,
Like roots below the frozen ground—
Still living,
Still holding the earth.

I do not ask why you stay.
You are here.
And that is enough.

Solitude

Stripped of luminosity,
A peak of evanescence,
Clouds begin to drift.

The moon arises,
Dancing the shadows,
A serenity that beguiles,
The perfect sense of nothing.

Echoes of the heart,
As twilight falls with eyes aglow,
A meadow engulfed by silence,
Where thoughts become undone.

A neutrality reserved
For solitary existence.

Oh, Heart

Oh heart, they say the soul is lost
When life has paid its final cost.
They say it fades like worn-out thread,
Unraveled slowly, then left for dead.

But heart, you've heard a different sound,
Like echoes humming underground.
When voices cease and hands go still,
You've felt what lingers, soft and real.

The shell may crack, the paint may peel,
The wheels may halt, the gears may kneel.
But something waits beyond the break,
A quiet pulse no end can take.

It sleeps beneath the weight of stone,
Not cold, not gone, just not yet known.
It holds a spark, it hums with grace,
And dreams of some far future place.

So when they say there's nothing more—
No distant light, no unseen door—
You answer not with proof or plan,
But with a truth the heart began.

The Apple Tree

One day
You will sit beneath a tree,
And apples will fall all around you.

They will hit the ground with weight,
Sweetness scattered on the earth
For those too afraid to reach.

Take one in your hand.
Feel its bruises,
Its beauty,
Its truth.

Not every apple is perfect,
But every one is real.

And the tree—
The tree keeps giving,
Without asking,
Without fear.

Marissa Harding

The Bird Within

A bird may leave the willow tree
And chase the open sky,
Yet some remain where roots run deep
And let the others fly.

It watches wings that cross the sea
And dreams of lands unknown,
But finds a peace in quiet limbs
And calls that space its own.

The cage is not of iron bars,
But made of softer things:
A branch familiar to the soul,
A hush beneath the wings.

I wondered once why birds stay still
When they are born to roam.
But then I looked inside my chest
And knew that I was home.

Two Years

Two years have passed,
A blur of days beneath a fading sky.
October's chill a bitter sting
Of leaves that softly fall.

Time moved
Like mist across the surface of a still pond.
Indifferent,
It slipped gently through the trees
As October shed her gold without concern.

The leaves fell
As things often do,
Without protest.

I remember your steadiness
As the pine remembers wind—
Not by sound,
But by the lean of its branches.

I left quietly
As dusk leaves the field,
Not to wound,
But to become shadow.

When I returned,
The ground had changed its name,
The path was overgrown,
But not unkind.

Now
I walk beside the stream,
Not to find what was lost,
But to sit in its echo.

The rain continues.
It does not mourn.

Marissa Harding

It simply falls,
And so do I,
Into the stillness
Of what remains.

Winter Without You

It is the stillness of December that wounds me most.
The frost arrives early in the morning,
Settling on the glass panes like memory—
Soft, persistent, and unwelcome.

The pine trees stand unadorned beyond the cabin window.
I have not the heart to string them with light.
A tree lit for no one feels more hollow
Than one left bare.

There is no fire in the hearth today,
Though the woodpile is full.
The hands that once kindled flame beside me
Are now committed to distance,
To duty perhaps, or to forgetting.

In the solitude of the woods
I find myself measuring absence more than time.
Each cardinal bright and indifferent,
Each icicle forming on the eaves,
Seems to ask, Where is your joy now?

I have written no cards.
To do so would make the silence real.
The stocking hangs limp,
Like an echo of joy I cannot reach.
Even the scent of cinnamon
Feels false without your breath beside it.

They say one must return to nature
To remember what is essential.
But what of love,
When love has wandered
And left no footprints in the snow?

You are not here.
And still the pond freezes over.

The fox slips through the trees.
The world remains unbearably beautiful
And utterly indifferent.

So this Christmas
There will be no feast,
No song,
No miracle.

Only the quiet
And the ache of a name
Not spoken aloud
Since the first frost.

The Quietest Release

How beautiful must dying be,
To rest within the ground
Where grasses whisper overhead
And roots are all around.

To hear the hush the silence makes
When every clock is still,
And feel no pull from yesterday
Nor chase tomorrow's will.

No need for thought or memory,
No sorrow left to keep,
Just folded in the gentle dark
As peaceful as in sleep.

The Last Rose

I laid a rose upon the stone,
Its weight no greater than a breath,
Its silence heavier than the years.

One stem, one bloom,
All I could carry into the dark.
I wanted it to speak your name,
But it only bent,
The way the living bend
When absence is too much to bear.

This was the last rose,
Fragile, defiant,
And still it could not cross
The distance between my hand and yours.

What Reminds Me Of Her

Sometimes it's the smell
Of spaghetti simmering slow,
Garlic rising like a hymn
From the stove that feeds a memory.

Sometimes it's a voice
With a certain twist of tongue,
The way they land their R's soft and proud,
And I hear her again,
Teaching me the words of my blood,
Praising me for getting it right.

She danced in the living room,
Barefoot and free,
Turning the floor into joy,
Laughing as if sorrow never met her.

Less than two years ago
She was here,
Shadowing my steps with grace,
Letting me play woman in her jewelry,
Letting me be little and loved.

And sometimes a scent,
Just a perfume in the air,
Brings me back to when I walked behind her,
Not yet knowing
What I would one day carry.

And sometimes a book
Makes me say, She would love this,
Until I remember
She can no longer tell me so.

But I remember,
Because she made sure I would.

Holding On

I held a handkerchief one day
And did not know quite why.
A memory clung soft to thread
As clouds would cling to sky.

The world became a distant sound,
Its edges not so clear.
The soul I sought in borrowed eyes
Was once too close, now near.

Some love remains beyond the flesh,
And hatred leaves its trace.
An absence presses on the stars
And darkens all of space.

A Bouquet For Mother

May springtime bloom where Heaven breathes,
And petals rise in prayer.
O Lord, I ask you gently now
To place your mercy there.

To send her what I cannot give—
A kiss upon her cheek,
An arm to hold her as she turns
With grace too pure to speak.

Her voice still hums in quiet rooms,
Her laughter in the shade.
But in my chest a hollow sings,
A pain that will not fade.

The Perched Soul

The path grew dim as I drew close,
And silence found its form.
The earth received my trembling tears,
No longer soft or warm.

The watchers wept in solemn rows,
The stillness wrapped the day.
I kissed your brow and let you go,
Though part of me would stay.

Your voice still lingers in my mind,
A sound I cannot lose.
And all my days I'd freely trade
For just one I could choose.

But now you rest with wings outspread,
Beyond where we can see.
And in your flight, I lost the part
That once completed me.

Of Scent And Sky

These feelings ride the scented breeze
And circle with the birds.
They stir within the morning hush
And rest in quiet words.

They rise with dusk on gentle wings,
Then fall like evening light,
And leave the soul too full to speak,
But not too full to write.

Marissa Harding

The Moon Brings Me Dreams

The moon ascends and brings me sleep,
But dreams it brings me too—
Of light that once adorned your face
And eyes of steady blue.

You were the song my spirit sang,
The breath beneath my prayer.
A hush remains when dawn departs,
And still I find you there.

I'd trade the gold of coming days
To hear your voice again.
The echo walks where memory dwells
And sweetens even pain.

No treasure blooms upon the earth
To match your quiet grace.
Your love still warms the folded space
Where time cannot erase.

You watch me from a gentler place
Beyond the veil of air,
Until the Lord should call for me
And place me in your care.

Beauty Like The Day

She wore beauty like the day—
Not fierce, not sudden,
But steady as morning light.

Her presence fell across the room,
And shadows softened.
Even her silence was a kindness,
Her laughter, a field in bloom.

I think of her now
As a rose kept in memory,
Unfaded by time,
Its fragrance still rising
Whenever I open the window of my heart.

Softly Comes The Day

The day arrives so silently,
It stirs the fields below.
A golden spill on morning's cloth,
Where sun and grasses grow.

Reflections wade in gentle lakes
As trees begin to yawn,
And leaves arise in quiet dance
To greet the coming dawn.

Gazing At The Stars

Above me the stars burned,
Each one a wound opening in the sky.
Their light fell into my hands
Like broken glass,
Sharp with memory.

I asked the night for an answer,
And it pressed its silence
Against my mouth.

In that silence I heard your breath,
The lost syllable of your name,
A river rising in the dark.

The stars did not console me.
They leaned closer,
Crowds of fire demanding
That I remember.

And still I remembered—
The warmth of your hand
Woven through my hair,
The way even absence
Leaves its shadow.

Dreams

I crave the dark,
The tender crook
Where dreams are softly kept.

They pass behind my shuttered lids
While waking thoughts have slept.

The sun may split the pane with light
Yet not disturb their place.
They echo down the silent halls
And never show their face.

My thoughts, they speak in foreign tongues,
My acts in beams of stage.
And all the truths I hide by day
Unfold upon that page.

The Heart

The heart, it is a fragile place,
But stronger than it seems.
It holds our passions, fears, and hopes,
And all our waking dreams.

It cannot live with treachery.
It starves when we deceive.
It asks for honesty alone,
And only that, believes.

Marissa Harding

The Cruel Beauty Of Music

How cruel that music dares to be
So beautiful, so bare.
It sings of loss and liberty,
Of things beyond repair.

It haunts with tones of aching love.
It weeps with pain's delight.
It paints the face of loneliness
In colors made of light.

It shows us joy, then turns away,
Yet leaves us wanting more.
The sweetest grief we ever knew
Still echoes at the door.

Have You Ever Really Loved Me

Have you ever really loved me,
Not with words but through the soul,
Where the sky turns colors inward
And the stars refuse control?

Have you missed me in the mirror,
Seen the ache inside my eyes?
Felt the rain beneath my spirit,
Where the quiet ocean lies?

Did you swim beneath the silence,
Did you plant your name in me?
Or drift past what could have flourished,
Lost in dreams that would not be?

Did your arms embrace the stillness,
Did your voice reach past the night?
Or am I alone in wonder,
Watching angels out of sight?

Growing Up To Find

Growing up and not yet knowing
What true love ought to be,
I gave and helped, but found too late
How much was lost in me.

I felt a fire inside my chest
For one who looked away,
And still I waited quietly
For him to choose to stay.

But time wore on and months grew thin,
The truth began to show—
That what I longed for most of all
Was never meant to grow.

I only meant to love him well,
But now I walk alone,
And wonder why the kindest hearts
So often turn to stone.

The Song That Stays

Play me a tune the way you've always done,
Slow at the start and finding pace with care.
Let every note fall honest, one by one,
Until the whole room knows the song is there.

The keys are worn where countless hands have been,
The black and white long molded to your own.
Your fingers move like memory through skin,
Each phrase a thing both borrowed and your own.

Your voice comes steady, close as someone's hand
That rests a while to show they mean to stay.
You sing of times I may not understand,
Yet still they find their way to me today.

So play it once for those who've gone away,
And once again for those who linger near.
A song's the kind of truth we let obey,
And still it stays long after we can hear.

That Girl Is Me

They told her hush.
They told her small.
They told her never rise at all.

But she is still here.
Her laughter cracks the glass in windows.
Her tears flood valleys and feed the roots.
Her steps are drums that wake the earth.

That girl is me,
The storm they feared would not obey,
The ember they could not smother.

I rise each morning unbroken.
My back is a pillar.
My tongue is a river.
My name is a bell that will not still.

Yes,
That girl is me,
And she is more than enough.

Come To Me

You have gone where my voice cannot follow.
Like a thought swallowed by silence,
You vanish before I can call you back.

Come to me from the place where you have hidden yourself.
Let me see your face without the veil of distance.
Here there is no judgment,
Only the truth that waits between us.

There is no need to carry your secrecy like a burden.
Lay it down.
Stand before me as you are.
Come to me, and I will meet you without fear.

Marissa Harding

She Walked Me Toward The Sun

An angel held me once,
And brushed away my tears.
She spoke of time in gentler terms
Than I had heard in years.

She turned my gaze toward morning light
And placed a dream inside.
Her voice became the budding branch
That wakes the countryside.

Through rain she was a steady hand,
Through storm, a sheltered flame.
She touched the air we lived within,
Yet never sought her name.

The whisper came, too soon, too still,
And took her from my view.
But in my heart she rises now
As every springtime new.

Safe Harbor

I have walked through nights without stars,
My steps uncertain,
My spirit searching for the place it belonged.

Every path was too narrow,
Every shelter too cold.
I did not know there was a home waiting for me
In the quiet chambers of another heart.

Here, no shadow crosses the threshold.
Here, the fears that once followed me
Are left at the door.
I am received without question,
And I rest in the presence of a love
That needs no proof.

It is not a touch that warms me,
But the knowing
That your spirit has met mine
And welcomed it without judgment.

It is not a kiss that soothes me,
But the way your heart
Has made a place for my own to live.

Now I can sleep as one who has found a safe harbor.
Now I can breathe in the quiet
Without fear of losing it.

My soul has been saved
Not by miracle or command,
But by the simple truth
Of love that holds fast and will not let go.

Renewal

When light dissolves the weight of night
The self, once hidden, opens wide
Memory loosens its quiet hold
And something unnamed begins to rise

A breath appears beyond all claims
As though the heart relearns its fire
Not by thunder, not by flame
But by the patience of desire

In absence lies a fertile hush
A hollow turning into song
Where even grief grows tender wings
And silence learns to carry on

Half-Finished Words

Your name sits cold in its bed of stone.
The letters gleam as if they could not hurt me.
I keep my hand there longer than I should,
Pressing the truth until my palm goes numb.

I try to sew the hours together,
But the thread frays and spills across the floor.
The empty space hums like a wound I cannot close.

I carry the half-finished words
We were meant to say.
They follow me into rooms I did not invite them to.
Even in my sleep, you do not leave.

The Shirt You Left Behind

It still hangs in the closet.
I touched it this morning.
The cloth gave nothing back.

I carried it to the chair.
Folded the sleeves over each other.
The collar was empty.

There is a stain at the cuff.
I wet it with soap.
It stayed.

The shirt dried by the window.
Wind moved through it.
For a moment I thought you breathed.

I put it away again.
The room did not change.
Only the silence grew heavier.

After The Fire

We danced
As if the floor had been written for us,
Our feet knowing what memory forgot.

You laughed,
But your hands trembled with truth,
Like leaves remembering the wind.

The door remained open.
You returned
With the quiet of returning rain.

I believed again,
With the soft ache of belief
That knows it is lying to itself.

You wore your suit like a question,
Pressed and polished,
But the ash of old fires
Still clung to your collar.

I smelled the ending before it spoke.
We spoke of forever
As if it could be touched,
Folded like linen.

But words are wind,
And wind does not stay.

I held the roof over us
With bare hands,
Carried the hours like water
In a cracked bowl.

You floated through me
As smoke does a room.
I stopped trying to revive

Marissa Harding

The ghost of your mouth,
Stopped counting
How often you almost loved me.

The lights we strung
Still hung in the fog,
Tired stars with nowhere to shine.

You never took them down.
But I did,
Because something must end
When nothing else will.

They called it strength,
But it was only silence,
The silence of not burning
For someone
Who feeds the fire and leaves.

You say I vanished,
But I was the last
Clinging to the ship's skeleton,
White-knuckled,
Cold as a shoreline
That forgets its name.

Two graves,
One gun.
You filled it with vows
That broke like glass in the dirt.
I buried them with my hands.

Now,
The color is returning to my sky.
Let the town keep its ghosts.
I no longer dig for our bones.

Desire

The fire has quieted,
But still the room is warm.
I do not chase it anymore,
That young hunger running wild
Through my veins.

Now desire comes slower,
A soft-footed guest.
It sits at my table,
Drinks from my glass,
Waits for me to notice.

There is grace in this too—
The hand that lingers,
The voice that does not rush.
Love does not need to shout
To be true.

I lay down in the gentled blaze,
And the embers keep me.
The body knows another kind of song:
Not fire,
But steady light.

Marissa Harding

The Quiet Work

The basket waits, a meadow of shirts and sheets.
We stand side by side,
Hands smoothing what the day has wrinkled.

Your sleeve finds mine,
And the room grows smaller,
The way a path narrows
When two sets of steps agree.

We fold the hours into neat piles,
The socks paired,
The towels stacked high.
Outside, the wind rattles its own disorder.

What is marriage if not this—
To take what is scattered,
To bring it together,
And call it ours.

The Phone Left Ringing

It rang in the other room.
I did not move.

The coffee cooled.
A fly traced the window.

When it stopped,
The house was the same house,
Only emptier.

When I Say Your Name

When I say your name
The sea lifts its shoulders,
The wind bends closer,
And the night scatters its coins of fire.

You are not only flesh,
You are the weight of rivers,
The patience of orchards,
The sky folded inside my chest.

When your voice reaches me,
It is not sound I receive,
But the opening of every silence,
A door thrown wide
Where I thought there was only stone.

Even the earth remembers you.
It opens its hands of soil and flame,
As if all creation conspired
To keep you near me.

If the world should fall,
If the stars abandon their posts,
I would still know your touch—
The first light,
Unextinguished.

Love Walks Among Us

Love rests in the chair still warm after rising,
In the apple split open,
In the path worn by countless feet.

It is the reason trees lean toward light,
The hush that follows rain,
The silence that gathers when two strangers
Lift their eyes at once.

Love builds no monuments.
It writes itself in small places—
A cracked cup still held,
A window opened for air,
A hand brushing the table
Before the door is closed.

We call it by many names,
But it needs none.
It has always been here,
Walking beside us,
Changing nothing into everything.

Part III – En Español

Abuela Me Dijo

Abuela me dijo:
Guarda pan para mañana,
Y también canciones.

El hambre se calma con un pedazo de pan,
El miedo con voz.

Abuela olía a café fuerte,
Y en sus brazos entendí
Que el corazón es una casa
Donde nunca se apaga la luz.

Calle Vacía

La calle se quedó con la risa de ayer.
Las ventanas bajaron sus párpados.

Camino sobre polvo,
Y levanto recuerdos,
Pájaros chiquitos de luz.

Nadie sale.
Sólo un mango madura callado,
Como la esperanza.

Amor Sencillo

Te amo en lo pequeño,
En la hoja que cae sin ruido,
En la gota de agua que enciende su brillo.

Te amo en lo inmenso,
En la noche que guarda sus astros,
En el mar que repite tu nombre.

No necesito adornos.
No necesito promesas.
En tu cuerpo encuentro el camino,
En tu voz,
El refugio donde la vida se salva.

Estar Enamorado

Es un fuego que no se apaga,
Mar que no se cansa de besar la orilla,
Flor que abre aunque el cielo tiemble.

Es caminar con el alma descalza,
Reírse mientras llueve caliente,
Sentir que el sol sale por sus ojos.

Es beso que cae como lluvia tibia,
Abrazo que encierra la paz de un sueño cumplido,
Orgullo rendido en su pecho.

Es buscar solo esas manos,
Guardar su calor como vida misma,
Y querer tanto
Que soltarlo sería dejar de respirar.

Si Algún Día Regresas

A veces me pregunto
Si tu corazón hablara
Igual que tu boca,
¿Tuvieras tanto miedo?

Hablas del amor como si ya se te hubiera ido,
Como si fuera cosa vieja,
Pero yo sé que tú lo sigues buscando,
Aunque no digas nada.

Sé que el pasado pesa
Y que confiar vuelve a doler,
Pero vivir pa' no sentir dolor
No es vivir tranquilo,
Es andar escondido del alma.

No te pido promesas
Ni palabras de novela,
Solo que no cierres la puerta
Como si nada valiera la pena.

Dios no da otra oportunidad
Pa' repetir lo mismo,
Sino pa' curar
Lo que todavía escuece.

Si algún día vienes,
Hazlo suave,
Sin orgullo,
Con la verdad por delante
Y el corazón sin trampa.

No sé si esto es destino,
Pero sé que el amor
No debe quedarse esperando
Afuera,

Pasando frío.

Yo estaré aquí,
Sin apuro,
Sin exigencias,
Solo con amor
Y esta vida que es mía,
Si tú la quieres compartir.

Disculpa

Se me fueron las promesas
Como agua tibia escapando de las manos,
Dejándome las palmas vacías y frías.

Te vi rota,
Pero guardé silencio,
Con la culpa amarrada al pecho
Como un collar de sal.

Te cargo en mi sombra,
Arropo tus lágrimas con mi voz,
Escondo tus cicatrices en la palma de mi mano,
Y sigues aquí,
Aunque yo me pierda entre brazos
Que nunca me quisieron.

Aunque mis palabras corten,
Nunca dejé de beber de tu fuerza,
Nunca dejé de creer
Que juntas podíamos alzarnos
Sobre la herida del mundo.

Otra Vez

Otra vez caigo en el mismo sitio,
Donde las paredes saben mi nombre
Y el suelo reconoce mis rodillas.

Tu sombra entra primero,
Mi corazón va detrás
Como un perro terco
Que no entiende
Que su dueño no regresa.

Las horas se doblan sobre sí mismas,
Como si el tiempo quisiera tapar
Que sigo aquí,
Esperando que tu voz me saque
De mis propios pensamientos.

Cada lágrima se pega a la piel
Como si quisiera quedarse a vivir.
Cada silencio crece
Hasta llenar la habitación entera.

Y si tu mano buscara la mía,
Todo este dolor
Sería un altar
Donde volvería a arrodillarme.

Todo Lo Que Tengo

Te he amado más de lo que debía,
Y en ese exceso me quedé desnuda por dentro.
A veces me protejo de tus palabras dulces
Porque sé que, si las dejo entrar,
Romperán lo poco que me sostiene.

Hay preguntas que se clavan
Como uñas en la carne.
Sé que las respuestas podrían matarme,
Y, aun así, las busco con hambre.

Te he dado tanto que era mío—
Mi cuerpo abierto,
Mi voz que te llama,
Mis pensamientos que te guardan.

Pero mi alma es lo único que no cedo,
Y mi corazón,
No lo toques.

Si suelto mi orgullo,
Me quedo sin refugio.
Si lo retengo,
Me quedo sola.

Camina,
Aunque yo me quede atrás,
Porque la luz seguirá encendida
Aunque mis manos ya no la cuiden.

Llévate lo que te ofrezco
Y no olvides que me importas,
Porque lo que pongo en tus manos
Es todo lo que tengo,
Y no hay más.

Alma Atormentada

Tu ausencia me abrió pasillos por dentro.
Camino a ciegas,
Con las manos raspando paredes vivas
Que sangran cuando las toco.

No hay muralla que detenga tu recuerdo.
Se cuela como agua sucia en la piedra,
Como un latido enfermo
Que no sabe rendirse.

Antes había un mapa en mi pecho.
Ahora es solo un papel mojado,
Con las rutas borradas
Y los nombres hundidos.

Todo lo que fui se derrumba hacia adentro,
Y quedo abrazando un silencio
Que pesa más que cualquier grito.

Me Digo A Mí Misma

Si encontrara el camino correcto,
¿Podría confiar en él sin dudar?
Si amara de verdad lo que hago,
¿Seguiría haciéndolo como hasta ahora?

He escuchado tus confesiones
Y conozco tus errores.
Pero aunque sé la respuesta,
No siempre me atrevo a decirla.
Porque hay verdades que se rompen
Si se pronuncian demasiado pronto.

La vida cambia sin avisar.
A veces lo que la transforma
Ya ha ocurrido,
Y solo nos damos cuenta
Cuando es demasiado tarde.

He aprendido que el alma puede resistir
Más de lo que cree.
Incluso cuando dice que no puede más,
Todavía guarda un último paso,
Un último aliento.

Crecer duele.
Cambiar quema.
Pero quedarse inmóvil
Es morir sin que nadie lo note.

Marissa Harding

Lo Que No Pueden Quitarme

Me revisaron hasta el alma
Buscando un permiso para existir.
Me miraron la boca
Esperando encontrar un país equivocado en mi voz.

Me preguntaron de dónde soy,
Y quise decirles:
Soy de donde mi abuela cantaba en la cocina,
De donde mi padre volvió con las manos partidas
Pero el pan completo.

No entendieron,
Solo buscaban papeles.

Si supieran que en mis bolsillos
Cargo la risa de mi gente,
El olor del café al amanecer,
La paciencia de quien sembró en tierra seca
Y dio fruto.

Pueden encerrarme,
Pueden negarme la entrada,
Pueden llamarme por un número,
Pero no pueden arrancarme
El mapa que llevo dibujado en la piel.

Ese mapa me guía
Incluso en la noche más oscura,
Incluso cuando el miedo me aprieta la garganta.

Que ellos se queden con sus leyes.
Yo me quedo con mi nombre.

Esta Tierra Que Piso

Crucé mares que tragaban sueños,
Y cielos que nunca aprendieron mi nombre.
Traía en la espalda el peso de mis muertos,
Y en las manos, la semilla de todo lo que no existía.

Esta tierra me recibió con un silencio antiguo,
Como si recordara a otros pies
Que también llegaron cansados
Y se atrevieron a quedarse.

Me dijeron que no era mía,
Que debía ganármela,
Como si el amanecer pidiera permiso para nacer,
Como si el río consultara su curso antes de abrazar la orilla.

Pero yo sé que pertenezco aquí,
Porque mi sudor hunde sus raíces en la misma tierra,
Y mi voz se quiebra con la misma sed
Que la de quien nació bajo este cielo.

No vine a robar, vine a sembrar.
No vine a callar, vine a cantar con el pecho abierto.
No vine a pedir comida, vine a compartir el pan entero,
Ese que sabe a trigo,
Y también a lágrimas.

Esta tierra no es un mapa,
Es un cuerpo que respira,
Y en cada aliento suyo
Late mi historia.

Si algún día me borran el nombre,
Si me arrancan las manos,
Si me cierran todas las puertas,
Me quedará la certeza más honda,
Que el polvo que soy y el polvo que piso
Son el mismo.

Marissa Harding

En La Isla Antes Del Trueno

El amanecer se abría como mango maduro,
Y la brisa traía el olor dulce de la caña.
Las palmas reales se estiraban tranquilas,
Guardando los caminos de tierra colorá.

En los portales, el café humeaba lento,
Y las voces eran bajitas, sin apuro.
Un gallo cantaba desde la finca vecina,
Y los guajiros, machete al hombro,
Iban marcando el paso al sol que subía.

En la plaza, las campanas llamaban a misa,
Y un vendedor de guarapo,
Con manos pegajosas de caña,
Sonreía sin prisa a cada cliente.

El mar, al fondo, venía con su murmullo de siempre,
Como si quisiera soltar un cuento largo
A quien se quedara oyendo.

La tierra estaba viva,
No de oro ni promesas de papel,
Sino de sudor y canto,
Y cada sombra sabía
El nombre de quien la pisaba.

Antes del trueno,
La isla era un corazón que latía sin miedo,
Y el tiempo, un río clarito
Donde todos bebían sin preguntar.

Flores De Verano

Las flores pintan la piel caliente de la tierra
Como si el cielo hubiera dejado caer oro líquido
Sobre los caminos, las lomas y los cañaverales.

Los árboles se levantan despacio,
Sus ramas buscan el aire alto,
Y allá arriba tejen un techo vivo donde la sombra respira.

Lluvia de oro cuelga en racimos brillantes,
Amarillo encendido que late sobre el verde,
Y la claridad se derrama por cada hoja
Como azúcar sobre fruta madura.

Faroles de pétalos flotan en la brisa,
Hablando en el idioma secreto del viento,
Mientras las hojas cuentan historias
Con un susurro suave y constante.

En las horas largas del calor,
El sereno de la madrugada queda abrazado a los palitos verdes.
La luz cae a través de las ramas
Y dibuja en el suelo mapas de fuego y sombra.

El sol derrama su filo y su caricia,
Y cada pétalo abierto es una moneda dorada
Que se gasta en el aire
Hasta perderse en la claridad de la tarde.

La brisa caliente y polvorienta recorre la llanura,
Trae el olor a hierba seca y tierra viva,
Y la espera silenciosa de la lluvia
Pesa sobre los campos como un secreto.

Las flores amarillas se mecen despacio,
Resplandeciendo bajo la espada encendida del verano,
Como si cada instante fuera el último día de luz.

El Susurro Del Otoño

Las nubes se arremolinan al filo del día,
Llamándose unas a otras antes que caiga la noche.
En el patio, el calor se quiebra de pronto,
Y una rana salta al canto mojado de la lluvia.

El verano todavía aprieta,
Pero el otoño ya se asoma,
Primero como un susurro pegado al borde del campo,
Después con manos de oro,
Pintando las hojas como si fueran retratos viejos.

Bajo mi ventana,
Una hoja solitaria cuelga de una telaraña,
Su brillo temblando como si supiera que le queda poco.
Un viejo duerme cerca,
Y en sus sueños se repiten los rostros
Que ya no vienen a visitarlo.

En el jardín,
Los crisantemos agachan la cabeza,
La tierra se viste de marrón cansado.
Los árboles sueltan su herencia al aire,
Y las hojas se confunden unas con otras,
Como vecinos que olvidan la frontera de sus patios.

Los pasos caen blandos sobre un camino de pétalos rosados,
Siguiendo un rastro que nadie ve,
Dando vueltas como hojas inquietas
En el espanto alegre de los gorriones.

Última Carta A Mi Cuba

Cuba mía,
Te escribo desde un cuarto ajeno,
Donde la luz no sabe tu color
Y las paredes no guardan mi voz.

No sé si mañana seguiré respirando,
Por eso hoy te lo digo todo.

Me arrancaron de tus brazos una madrugada,
Y desde entonces camino como sombra
Por calles que no me pronuncian el nombre.

Aquí nadie entiende que mi corazón
Sigue latiendo con el ritmo de tus tambores,
Ni que mi sangre huele
A café recién colado.

Recuerdo tus madrugadas lentas,
Cuando el gallo rompía la noche
Y la brisa traía promesas de café.

Recuerdo la risa de mi padre
Jugando dominó bajo un farol,
Las voces de la radio
Cantando Benny Moré,
Y los almendrones brillando en la calle
Mientras el humo de un tabaco
Se mezclaba con el olor del pan caliente.

Todo eso me lo guardé en el alma
Como quien guarda pan para no morir de hambre.

He visto mares y montañas extranjeras,
Pero ninguno me ha devuelto
El peso dulce de tu calor.

En este suelo prestado

Marissa Harding

Las flores no saben decir mi nombre
Y el cielo me mira como si no me conociera.

Cuba, si esta es mi última noche,
Quiero que sepas que me muero de amor por ti.
Que cada lágrima que derramé lejos de ti
Fue un puente invisible para volver.
Que nunca aprendí a soltarte,
Ni quise.

Si alguna vez el viento te trae mi voz,
Déjala correr por tus calles,
Déjala posarse en los balcones,
Déjala dormir junto al mar.

Quiero que mi último aliento
Se mezcle con tu aire
Y que, aunque mis huesos queden aquí,
Mi alma regrese
A casa.

Regreso Imposible

He vuelto,
Pero no he vuelto.

La calle cambió su sombra,
El aire lleva otro canto.
Las casas me miran en silencio,
Como si yo fuera el extraño.

El mar dice mi nombre,
Pero con otra voz,
Más cansada, más lejana.

Camino con la llave en la mano.
La puerta no responde.
Sólo mi pecho guarda la isla
Que ya no existe afuera.

Part IV – The Body Remembers

Taken

I was a child
With questions still forming,
With skin that had never learned
What it meant to flinch.

He came like silence,
Not with thunder,
But with a quiet
That swallowed
Everything bright.

My voice was a bird
Too small to lift its wings.
My body,
A map redrawn
Without my knowing.

I did not bleed,
Not in the way they ask,
But something broke
Beneath the surface
And learned how to stay quiet.

For years,
I carried a name
That was not mine,
Shaped by hands
That never asked permission.

But here,
In this line,
In this breath,
In this truth spoken aloud
For no one but myself,
I begin again.

I did not invite the storm.

I was the roof that held through it.
And though the rafters shook,
I remained.

Now, I write the body back.
I name what was mine
Before it was taken,
And I keep walking
Into a light that does not burn.

No One Asked

It was pink once.
The room.
The body.
The part of me that knew nothing.

He did not break in.
He belonged.
He smiled.
That was the trick.

I became wallpaper.
Something still.
Quiet.
Striped in shame.

No blood.
No sound.
Only the ceiling
Watching like a pale-eyed god.

Afterward,
My shadow grew teeth.
My hands became strangers.
I folded my name
Into smaller and smaller letters
Until it vanished in my throat.

No one asked.
No one ever asks.

I grew up around it.
I dressed it in normal.
I covered it with years.

But it never left.
It hummed under my ribs.
It clung to my wrists

When no one was looking.

This is not a story
For clean hands.
This is a story
Stitched into bone.

I was a girl.
He was not.
That is all.
And it is everything.

Shadowed Self

A shadow moves inside my skin.
It lies down when I lie down.
It rises when I rise.
It keeps its mouth pressed against my breath.

I cannot peel it away.
Its hands are stitched to my own.
Its voice hums under my tongue,
A wasp caught in sugar.

At night it grows enormous,
Covering the walls like black water.
I reach for the lamp, but the light bends.
It does not touch me.

This shadow is not a stranger.
It is the child I abandoned in the mirror.
It is the silence that learned my name
And refuses to leave.

Marissa Harding

The House In My Throat

There is a house in my throat,
And every morning it screams.
The rooms breathe panic,
Barefoot, toothless, gasping.

I hold my tongue like a blade.
The day won't bleed right.
My ribs are attic beams,
Groaning under the weight of thoughts
That nest like birds with rusted claws.

They do not sing.
They scratch and scratch
Until even my silence leaks noise.

I brush my teeth with fear.
Eat breakfast like a dare.
Make my bed for the ghosts.
Try to leave the house
Inside my throat,
But the door won't open.

This Morning I Couldn't

This morning I couldn't get out of bed.
The room was quiet.
The walls were kind.
But I couldn't.

The coffee was made.
Black.
Strong.
I drank it, and still
It was there—
The weight,
The knot,
The thing with no name.

I smoked a cigarette I didn't want.
Felt nothing.

Went for a walk
Because walking is what we do
When we can't speak,
When there's no one to ask
What silence means.

The street was clean.
The sky was tired.
The world was fine.
The world didn't care.
That helped.

I Felt A Panic Crouch Inside

I felt a panic crouch inside,
A thing with greedy claws.
It did not knock or beg to stay.
It slipped beyond the laws.

It sat and watched my shallow breath.
It whispered I was not.
It tightened every windowpane
And every key I'd lost.

I wrote a letter to the air,
But it refused to read.
The soul escapes so quietly
When strangled by its need.

His Words Lived In My Mouth

His words lived in my mouth
Like spoiled milk, curdling
Each time I tried to speak.

They nested behind my teeth,
Heavy with judgment,
Light enough to slip in while I slept.

He called me glass,
Then stepped hard.
Said I was too much
And not enough
In the same breath.

A magician of cruelty,
Pulling shame from empty places.

I learned not to echo.
My voice was not a tool
But a wound.

Even now,
I spit shadows
When I try to say my name.

And Still, I Heard Him

He did not raise a hand.
No, not once.
He raised his voice,
And that was enough
To pull the sky from under me.

He called me names
As if he had the right
To rename my bones.
Told me I was too much,
Too angry,
Too bold,
Too wrong.

And I listened,
Because I thought love meant listening,
Even when it hurt.

But one day
I gathered myself,
The way women do,
With hands that remember softness
And strength.

And I said—
No.

He called again.
I did not answer.
He spoke again.
I did not bend.

And the silence between us
Was the first thing
I ever owned.

What He Said Was Not The End

When he spoke,
He tried to unmake me,
Tried to fracture my face
With phrases,
Slice my power
Into parts.

I counted the times
He said,
You are crazy.
You are too much.
You are imagining it.
Until I stopped counting.
Until I stopped believing.
Until I started writing it down.

My rage is not fragile.
My memory is not faulty.
My softness is not an invitation
For erasure.

I survived each syllable
He weaponized.
And now,
When I speak,
I do it
With the weight
Of every woman
Who ever swallowed a scream
And still sang.

Undone

The tongue is a serpent in a glove of pearls.
It dances, unseen, and uncoils ruin
Without the mercy of red.

Thoughts drift like bruised paper lanterns
Through the attic of the skull.
We are stitched from their smoke,
From their murmurs in the wallpaper.

When the mind is rinsed clean—
A cathedral of snow and bone—
Joy arrives barefoot,
Trailing silver threads,
And follows us
Like a mirror turned toward the sun
That refuses to dim.

I Kept The Blade Close

There was a rhythm in it,
A silence after the noise,
Like snow over a screaming field.

The blade didn't lie.
It was cold, and it stayed cold
While everyone else warmed themselves
On my absence.

I made red windows in my skin
To look out from the inside,
Because mirrors betrayed me
And words broke apart like glass in the mouth.

They said,
Don't do this,
But no one noticed when I stopped speaking—
Only when I started bleeding,
The color they understood.

Even now
I miss the silence it gave me,
The quiet, the control,
The feeling of nothing
Becoming something I could see.

Wounds In Stillness

They say the woods are healing,
But I walked there once
Carrying a knife in my pocket
And silence in my chest.

There were no birds,
Only wind
And the sound of my own pulse
Begging me to do it again.

I did not seek peace.
I sought proof
That I was real,
That I could cut through the fog
Inside my ribs.

The trees stood
And watched
And said nothing.

And when it was done,
My skin stung like memory,
And I walked back
Less
Than I had been.

A Song The Body Sang

I carved a song into my arms
Because no one listened
When I whispered.

I opened my skin
Not to die
But to disappear,
One layer at a time.

The blood told stories
My mouth was too ashamed to speak.
It sang softly
In the bathroom,
On the floor,
Behind locked doors.
It sang until I could not hear myself.

They called it a phase,
A cry for help.
But I was not crying.
I was cutting
Because the pain was quieter
Than the rage.

This Is Not A Metaphor

This is not poetry.
This is not a metaphor.
These were blades.
These were lines.
These were hours I lost to the sharp edge
Because no one heard what I never said.

I used razors like punctuation
To end the sentence of a day,
To pause the shame,
To slice the noise,
To control the flood.

Do not call it a moment.
Do not make it soft.
It was the only place
I could place the pain
Without being told
I was imagining it.

Even the mirror
Refused to look at me.

And still
I pressed the steel,
Because at least
That hurt
The way it was supposed to.

The Weight Of Wanting Less

I went to the woods to vanish in plain sight.
Not to find God,
But to lose the evidence of myself.

The pines stood tall in their certainty
While I measured each mouthful
Like contraband I could not afford to be caught with.
I feared the riot of my own flesh
If I stopped guarding the gates.

I told no one,
Except the branches that bent to listen,
That I wore my body like an accusation
I could never defend against.

The forest bore witness
As I receded past skin and voice,
Slipping into a version of myself
That did not cast a shadow,
Only the faint percussion of a heart
Still insisting on being here.

I Fed Myself Nothing

I fed myself nothing
And still felt too full,
Not with food
But with shame.

A shame that clung to my thighs,
Whispered behind my spine.

I wore baggy clothes
Not for style,
But to drown the outline of me,
To pretend I was not a thing
To be looked at,
Or judged,
Or touched.

I smiled when they said,
You're so thin,
And cried
Because they meant it.

I stared at plates
As if they could forgive me
For what I was.

They never did.

My Body Is A War I Was Taught To Lose

A war scripted for me by mouths that looked like mine,
By hands that claimed they were feeding me
While spooning in shame like medicine I did not ask for.

It was inheritance—
The kind that steals your name and calls it tradition.
It lived in the eyes that weighed me,
In photographs where I was already disappearing,
In the quiet that followed when I took up too much space.

They said love yourself,
But only in fractions.
They said health,
But meant compliance.
They said beautiful,
But demanded my ribs sign the contract first.

So I learned to swallow myself,
To fold my hunger into obedience
Until I could not tell the difference between appetite and sin.

The mirror became my warden.
The plate, a negotiation table where I always lost.
The compliment, a loaded weapon disguised as kindness.

Do not speak to me of peace.
Peace does not live in the mouths of those
Who taught me to harm myself for their comfort.

Peace will come
Only when I am no longer performing survival
In a costume they approve of.

Marissa Harding

He Taught Me Silence With His Hands

He did not lift the child
But the walls.
The air became a shout,
And the shout became a hand,
And the hand became a stone.

I learned the stillness of floors,
The breathless watch of hinges,
The alphabet of footsteps.

My name turned iron in his mouth,
A bell struck only for blame,
Never for blessing.

They say hate devours its keeper,
Yet he dined first.
The child was a morsel,
The husk a remnant
Cast aside in sound and shadow.

And now the closing of wood,
The fall of air against a frame,
Folds me back into that small room
Where nothing happened,
And nothing was all there was.

He Was The First Cage

He was the first cage.
The morning fear,
The shadow before the sun.

His voice bent my spirit low,
Told me my laugh was thunder,
My steps an earthquake,
My self a crime.

He wrapped himself in the word father
Like it was a robe of light.
But I had seen the lining,
And it was ash.

His silence was a whip,
His words the crack.
He watched my shrinking and called it honor.

So I learned the art of vanishing.
I locked my wants away,
Tucked my hope behind my ribs.

For in his house,
To be seen was to be struck.

There was no love in that kingdom,
Only commandments carved in stone.

And still, I was the rebel child,
Breaking his law
Each time I drew breath.

Marissa Harding

I Do Not Call Him Father

I do not call him father.
The language refuses him.
It is a soil he salted,
A prayer he broke between his teeth
And spat back into the mouths of children.

He returned from the world
Carrying not bread
But the smell of threat.
And I, still soft with milk,
Learned the weight of footsteps
The way some learn lullabies.

I was not born to vanish,
But I became a disappearing act,
Pressed thin against walls,
Learning the shape of quiet
Until quiet had my name.

His hands were empty
Of every form of mercy.
Even his silence was a blade.

I knew I hated him
Before hate became a word in my mouth.
And now that I own my tongue
I will not spend it on him.

Self-Destruction

There are mornings when I wake in a house I do not recognize,
Though my hands have built every wall.
It is filled with the smell of burnt paper
And the heavy breath of something waiting.

I can tell you I feel sadness but never hatred,
That laughter sometimes escapes me like a moth through a crack,
But the truth is my skin is stitched with hunger
And I have been split along the seam.

I have learned to drag my body forward
Through the muck of my own thoughts,
To work and to play
And to nail my mistakes to the page like butterflies.

I can name the strangers who have walked through me,
The things I have seen,
The things I will see,
But I cannot loosen the noose I have tied for myself.

There are nights when I drop to my knees,
Palms pressed to the floorboards,
Feeling the tremor of my own breath.

I count the small proofs that I am alive—
The scrape of my nails,
The ache in my back,
The taste of metal in my mouth.

And still I turn inward
To the corner where my own reflection
Waits with its patient scorn.

I call this not forgiving myself.
I call this a depression that waits in the corner
Like a quiet executioner.

Marissa Harding

It is the slow burning of my own life
While I am the one striking the match.

If I cannot make you understand,
Then I will show you the tear
And let you watch it fall.

Left Behind

The light bends around her face as if it does not want to touch her,
Sliding away in thin streams while the shadows close in.

Tears cling to her skin,
Not falling,
As though the weight of them is enough to keep her in place.

The room smells of sweat and a wrongness that will not speak its name.
My father's voice is sharp and cutting,
A tool meant to wound before the hands arrive.

Those hands write their violence into my skin,
A language of power and ownership.
It teaches me to become small,
To hide my breath inside my ribs.

My mother is still in the house
But already far away.
Work pulls her out the door,
And when she returns
She carries her own bruises,
Some visible, some buried under her sleeves.

I know the same hands that strike me have struck her.
We are two bodies kept in the same cage,
Each learning to survive in different corners.

I am thirteen
And already fluent in the pauses before anger,
The footsteps that mean I should not be seen,
The weight of silence before a blow.

My pillow becomes my only witness,
Drinking in what I cannot say.

I watch my mother's back as she leaves again.
I feel my father's grip pull me closer.

There is no trust in the words he speaks,
Only the threat beneath them.

Some part of me knows
We have both been left behind,
Even while we are still here.

Leave Me Alone

Your words arrive like stones dropped into my hands,
And you expect me to hold them without flinching.

You say them lightly,
As though advice were a ribbon you could tie around me and call it a gift.

I have listened.
I do not agree.

I once told myself the same things you say now.
I thought change could be commanded
Like light turned on in a locked room.

Then I learned that some rooms have no key.
You have not lived my days.
You have not carried the weight that presses my bones into the ground.

I am not cold.
I am wondering why my skin feels raw beneath the air.
Perhaps it is the stress breaking through its surface,
The weight I have worn so long
That my body has forgotten it is there.

She comes again,
The shape I know as depression.
She watches me from the corner
With the patience of a predator.

I could walk to her.
I could remain still.
Either way she will strip me down
To the hollow she prefers.

I think of the years when she was absent,
How the air was clearer,
How I could lift my head without effort.
But my past self opens the door when I am not watching

And lets her step in as though she belongs.

Now another figure stands beside me,
Different in face but made of the same substance.
Perhaps this is a test.
Perhaps it is a reminder
That if I am to rise,
I must hold myself upright
Before anyone else can.

Silent Pain

The storm tears across the desert,
Its mouth full of sand and broken glass.

I stand in its center,
Stitched with memories
That gnaw at my ribs.

Rain claws at my clothes
Until they hang in strips.
Wind slices my skin
In lines that burn long after it passes.

Loneliness lingers in my mouth—
Sharp, metallic,
Like something bitten by mistake.

I think of love,
How I held it in both hands
And still watched it fall through.

The thought of living without it
Presses against my chest like stone,
Yet the thought of ending
Is heavier still.

I stand at the mouth of the abyss.
If I stepped forward,
Pain would fall away like clothes.
But my feet root in the dust,
Held by a thread of will.

The storm breaks.
First light cuts the horizon,
A pale warmth touching my face.

For a moment
I believe it.

The Wound That Waits

I keep my place at the table's far edge,
Where words do not reach.
Laughter blooms in the center,
But its petals never touch me.

Your back is a locked gate.
I know its hinges will never turn,
Yet I stand at it daily,
Hands quiet at my sides.

They pass me as if I were dust on the floor,
Too small to see, too common to notice.
Better that than their painted kindness,
The counterfeit clasp of their hands.

Still, there is a wound that waits
For your eyes to find it,
For your voice to name me
Before I disappear entirely.

My Shadow Stays With Me

There are days when the mind is heavy,
And the weight will not shift.
Thoughts move like slow rivers,
Twisting into corners I did not build.

I sit with memories,
Their edges still sharp,
And wonder where the hurt began.
Maybe with one tear,
A small thing,
But strong enough to pull me under.

I think of a creature fighting a current
It could not beat,
Sold away for so little
That even the story was lost.

I look at my hands.
The fingers slip from me,
Crawl toward something they remember.
What can a body do alone
Except keep reaching for what is gone?

Now the words come without me.
They know my truth,
They travel my mind like they built it.

I learn I can fall as well as rise,
Sink into what has been thrown away
And find pieces that still belong to me.

I could be swallowed by the old clothes in the closet,
The ones that still smell of another life.
My hair is gone.
My hands are tired.

So I sit in the farthest corner

And speak to the only thing that will listen.
My shadow stays with me,
And when I cry,
It cries too.

When It Comes

I know the shadow that waits for me.
It walks without hurry,
Its feet finding my footprints
As if the road belongs to us both.

It does not whisper.
It does not shout.
It stands in my doorway
When the night closes in.

I have seen it dressed in black silk,
As if grief could be made elegant.
I have felt its hand hover above my shoulder,
Weighing the moment,
Measuring my breath.

The morning may come late.
The clocks may hold their tongue,
And the buildings may lean like tired giants.
But I still rise to meet the day.
I still breathe the air that was meant for me.

When it comes,
And it will come,
I will not greet it on my knees.
I will stand in the open light,
Wrap my courage around my shoulders,
And walk toward it
As though I have been ready
All my life.

Part V – The World As It Is Broken

A Cracked Glass

This world—
A cracked glass.
Reflects war back at itself,
Shattered over blood and bone,
Where breath is bargaining chip
And innocence means nothing.

The sky learns to scream.
Warplanes carve their rage into air.
Missiles spit thunder.
And somewhere,
A home forgets how to be a home.
Smoke sings louder than lullabies.

Children,
With eyes too quiet,
Mouths too still,
Hearts spilling red tears,
Learn what silence cannot save
And what it cannot name.

A mother rocks empty space
Between her arms.
A wife folds absence like a dress
That no longer fits.
A man carries grief like a stone
Tied behind his teeth.
A child cries out for the unreturnable.

We call it sacrifice.
We dress it up in ceremony.
But this is loss.
This is theft.
This is hatred grinning in the face of mourning.

Hatred is a slow poison,
Fed in daily doses.

Marissa Harding

It creeps, it curls, it waits,
Like cancer with teeth,
Like shadows that cut at the spine,
Like history repeating,
And repeating,
And repeating.

You want to find peace here?
Then name what we've become.
Name what we've allowed.
Name what must end
Before the mirror breaks us all.

Quiet Hours

In the quiet hours, the wound is hidden.
Curtains close,
The neighbors look away.
History is written in whispers
Too soft to shame the guilty.

Yet silence is never empty.
It gathers like smoke,
It shouts louder than guns.

This is the silence of witnesses,
The silence of fear called peace.
Stones remember what men forget.
Their silence is heavier than graves.

I will not keep it.
I will not let their quiet
Become my own.

The Fire I Chose

Solitude was given,
But the door stayed shut.

Sin trailed me
Like breath in winter.

His eyes were iron.
The years would not bend.

I erased the world
To crown the one I invented.

Some did not know.
One did.

Be the fire you beg for.
I will not drink from the mouth
That burned me.

Love rose when I chose myself.

Still he sees her
As if light had chosen his face.

His voice carries
Every room he has died in
And left standing.

The Ribbon

The black ribbon gleams,
A slit vein in the throat of the earth.
It pulls, it whispers—
Not a road,
A command.

Something unseen insists follow.
I obey,
Barefoot, bright-eyed,
Aching toward light unborn.

Behind me mountains,
Crushed knuckles of the planet,
Bruised and rising from the boil.
Their wounds never close.
Fractures run deep,
Etched in silence.
She gives no comfort,
But I am allowed.
We run.

Steel bones grow through her,
Wooden signs, rusted names.
They say hope city arrival,
But I know
These are just words for want.

The sky, riddled with neon lies,
Burns like paper touched by breath.
I do not believe it.
The ribbon curves its spine.
I kneel
And run.

We are hearts forgotten,
Buried before we beat.
Time loops like a snake,

Marissa Harding

Tail in mouth,
Always returning
To the place we began
And never asked for.

The seasons hum their grief,
Not songs but whimpers
With mother-salt on their tongues.

I run.
Still.
The black ribbon glimmers,
Its lure eternal.
It winds ahead,
Deep into the bone of night.

It does not promise.
It does not end.
Only forward,
Until I break
And can run no more.

Long Forgotten

I lay my soul here as one lays down a wounded child
And ask the dark to keep it still.
I would leap if it meant the weight would loosen
And those I love could be left untouched.

The promise I once made to you sleeps in me,
Sealed inside a chamber no one enters.
Your voice is etched into my marrow,
And even silence cannot erase it.

The sun rises as though it has not heard my plea.
Its light is cruel,
Its heat bites into my pale skin until it blooms red.

In this bright and merciless world
I rest like a shadow pinned in place.

My grave is only stone and words,
But it cradles me better than any embrace.
The ground is empty,
Yet I know its language,
The slow pulse of nothingness that feels almost like peace.

Anything is better than the hollow stare of a life half-lived.
The years I endured have grown into something
I no longer recognize as mine.

There is a moment when the body loosens its hold
And the spirit leans forward.
I listen for the stillness I have begged for,
But it comes dressed in echoes,
Voices that cannot reach me.

I feel the shadow of someone searching,
Though I cannot meet their eyes.
It is too late for that kind of rescue.
I kneel before the same pain

That has always owned me,
Its hands resting on my shoulders like a crown.

I wait for it to show its face.
I wait alone,
And the waiting becomes eternity.

Will anyone ever break the code of my words,
Or will I remain an alien
To a world that makes me smaller each day?

I tell fate my final secrets
And wonder if it ever loved me at all,
Or only when it was stealing my mind.

Silence

Silence is the neighbor of every star.
It holds them in its dark embrace,
Burning yet unspoken.

I press my ear to the night.
The silence enters me,
A river without water,
A mouth without breath.

It is the hymn the universe keeps,
Older than grief,
Greater than me,
A secret name spoken only to itself.

The Island I Carry

In the warm hush of evening,
I remember streets washed in gold,
Where shutters whispered secrets
To the sway of palm shadows.

The air was thick with guava and tobacco,
Laughter spilling from open doorways
Like the rum in an uncle's glass.

Somewhere, a radio crooned a bolero,
And the slow strum of a tres
Wandered into every heart.

I see my mother at the window,
Her hands kneading dough,
The scent of bread rising
To meet the salt from the sea.

Children chased the day's last light
Past domino tables on the corner,
Their shouts stitched into the fabric of dusk.

Now oceans away,
I carry that island in my chest—
Its colors, its music,
Its quiet promise before the storm.

And in dreams,
I walk those streets again,
Barefoot and certain
The night would never fall.

The Angel Sings Against The Dark

A tender seed begins to grow,
Already bent with pain.
The root is deep in barren ground,
And thirst will come again.

A need that burns within the chest
No water can release,
A wish for hands to lift the weight
And give the spirit peace.

But hate has wound its careful web
Around the open heart.
It keeps the voice from speaking hope,
It pulls the soul apart.

An angel sings against the dark,
Her song is small and clear.
And though the chains still hold their grip,
The heart leans in to hear.

The Fragile Place

The heart wept through the empty night,
Its wings cut close to bone.
It sought a dawn that might erase
The ache it called its own.

Through fire it passed to find release
From weight too sharp to bear,
And thought the hand that ends a life
Might meet it kindly there.

A rose was held against the breast,
Its perfume soft and near,
Till petals fell to earth that waits
For all it loves to hear.

Yet still the breath returned once more,
Though grief had pled its case.
And in the ashes left behind,
Love held its fragile place.

Ashes In The Wind

The village burned.
Walls fell into themselves,
And the earth glowed with sorrow.

But the smoke rose higher than the flames.
It carried their names,
Their songs,
Their unspoken prayers.

Even now,
You can taste them in the wind.
The body remembers.
The spirit does not vanish.

Gunfire Psalm

After the noise,
The room remembers.

Desks hold the heat of hands
That will not return.
A book lies open,
Its question unanswered.

Do not give me thoughts.
Do not hand me prayers
Wrapped in silence.

We need a law that loves our children
More than our fear.

The chalk waits at the board.
It is not holy.
It is not enough.

The Ground Changes

Another explosion split the night.
The sky burned and the earth shook,
And from the smoke rose a cry
For the living and the buried.

Hands reached through rubble,
Pulling breath from stone.
Rain fell on their shoulders
And faces lifted upward,
Waiting for something greater than water.

I have seen eyes that have learned not to trust.
I have seen shame without a face.
I have seen a people rise in one breath,
As if freedom had broken the lock of the hour.

Soldiers keep their silence.
Journalists guard small flames.
One smile survives.
A statue falls.
A branch is lifted against the dust.

And from the ruin, a voice:
We have been counted as shadows,
But today the world will see our faces.
We have been given reason to bow,
But today we will stand.
We have been left with only the earth,
And now the earth is ours.

No wall can outlast the will of a people.
No fire can consume the truth of their breath.
When the living stand together,
The ground changes.
And when the ground changes,
The world must follow.

Floodplain

The river rose and took the fence in pieces.
We stacked our photographs on the piano bench
And watched the yard turn lake.

A neighbor rowed by,
His hat resting in his lap.
He said water has a good memory.
We nodded,
And did not look at each other.

When the sun came back,
The mud wrote its lines across the floor.
We read them,
And said nothing.

The Refugee's Shoes

On the shore a pair of shoes waits.
Salt has whitened the leather
Until it shines like bone.

No feet return to claim them.
They stand open
Like questions without answers.

Who walked in them across the dark?
Who carried a heartbeat for an oar,
A child for a star?

The sea knows.
It keeps the names in its wide mouth.
The shoes wait still,
A prayer abandoned at the water's edge.

Border Crossing

A child presses her fingers
Through the wire's small squares.
She counts them
Like beads of a prayer
No one taught her.

The sun does not ask for papers.
The wind carries no flag.
But men with guns
Stand between her and tomorrow.

Call it border,
Call it law.
I call it hunger fenced in steel.
I call it cruelty
That dares to name itself order.

Her eyes are the crossing.
Her breath is the future.
And no wall is high enough
To outlast her need to live.

Pandemic Morning

We learned the weight of breath,
How it trembles in the body
Like a secret flame.

We measured distance in love,
Keeping apart so we might keep each other.
Windows became altars.
Hands remembered water as blessing.

In the hush of those mornings
We heard our names again,
Spoken by small lamps
We kept for one another.

Extinction Song

A thin note in the trees
Waiting for reply.
The meadow holds its breath.
The sky does not answer.

Feathers remember flight.
Wings forget the air.
What vanishes in silence
Still leaves a cry.

City Protest

We filled the street with our breath.
One voice called,
Another answered,
And the city learned our song.

We spoke the names
They tried to bury.
We lifted them higher
Than sirens,
Higher than guns.

This is not noise.
This is not chaos.
This is the sound of living.
This is the sound of a people
Who will not be erased.

Letter To The Future

Children not yet born,
Forgive us our sleeping.
We mistook comfort for truth,
And profit for breath.

We cut the forests into silence.
We fed the sky with smoke.
We taught the rivers
To carry our poisons.

And still you are coming,
Bright as unbroken dawn.
Take from us what we could not finish.
Take from us the fragile earth,
Still alive enough to love you back.

May your hands be wiser than our hunger.
May your voices rise louder than our greed.
And may you walk unafraid
In a garden we could only imagine.

The Crop Of War

The ground does not sleep.
It drinks what we pour into it,
Hour by hour.

Roots learn the taste of metal and ash
And hold it in their thin mouths.

While here we tend another garden,
Pulling water from clean pipes,
Feeding the green we call home.

Elsewhere the night is red,
And history's hunger cracks the soil.
Bombs split the sky
And write their bright
And brutal scripture across the dark.

Air thick with the dust of people,
Ground packed with the pulp of memory,
Children born into the taste of poison,
Their veins carrying
The slow instructions of death.

War is not an accident.
It is a crop we have planted
And fed.

Its roots run deep into the marrow of the planet,
Pulling from every century
The same nutrients of fear and greed.

We will eat this fruit
Again and again
Until we tear the root from the earth
And burn the seed in our own hands.

Part VI – Toward Light

A Call From Death

I called and death responded slow,
As if he heard a hymn.
Yet when his shadow crossed the door
The light grew pale and dim.

I thought to step within his room
And end the aching years,
But at his threshold felt the breath
Of unimagined fears.

Perhaps the heart can beat again
Without the shroud of dread.
Perhaps the blood recall its course
And warm the frozen thread.

So death stood silent at my gate,
His hand upon the latch.
I turned and let the living sun
Unfasten its own catch.

The Scar Speaks

I am the seam the fire forgot to hide.
Once I was blood's river,
Once I was the mouth of pain.

Now I am silver,
A thin thread across the skin.
I do not close.
I remember.

Do not call me ugly.
I am a grammar of survival,
A mark the body keeps
So the mind will not forget.

Touch me,
And you will feel a history
Pressed into silence.
Touch me,
And you will know
What endured.

Therapy Session

The chair was plain.
I sat in it.
The clock moved but did not hurry.

I spoke.
Then I stopped.
The room held the words.

Between us was quiet.
It did not accuse.
It did not forgive.

A plant leaned toward the window.
I watched it.
It seemed enough.

Dancing After

The music begins,
And the room forgives me.
My feet remember joy
In their old bones.

I turn, and the air turns softer.
I rise,
A flame that will not be hidden.

This body was once a battlefield.
Now it is a drum.
Now it is a song.

What tried to break me
Learns my rhythm
And falls behind.

I dance,
And the world opens its arms.
I dance,
And I am whole again.

The First Morning Without Fear

The sun arrived as if it had always been here.
Grass lifted its heads,
The earth loosened its breath.

Children opened the door
And did not look behind them.
Their laughter rose like smoke,
But it was not from fire.

Even the stones grew lighter,
Their silence no longer heavy.
The air itself became a garment,
And it fit.

I cupped my hands to the stillness.
It was not emptiness.
It was the sound of peace,
Spoken for the first time.

Hands Open

I carried my fists through the years.
They were heavy.
They kept me alone.

Today I let them fall.
I lift my hands to the air.
It moves through me.
It blesses me.

These hands are not closed anymore.
They welcome.
They reach.
They rise.

Come here, world.
I am ready to hold you.
I am ready to be held.

Joy Is Also A Weapon

They told us sorrow was the only song.
They told us rage was our only tongue.

But we learned another grammar.
We dressed in color.
We laughed in the teeth of grief.
We fed each other bread still warm.

Joy is not escape.
It is the sharpened edge of living.
It is the refusal to be erased.

Call it weapon if you must.
I call it survival in bright clothes,
The unbroken music of the heart.

Light Is A Language

Light speaks without words.
It writes across the wall,
It writes across the skin.

It names the river,
The stone, the child,
And they answer.

In the bowl of morning
The sacred water shines.
I drink,
And the day moves through me like song.

What was broken begins to mend.
What was hidden begins to rise.

Light is a language older than fear.
Today, I am fluent.

Cathedral Of Breath

Morning arrives already singing.
The air moves through me not as guest but as kin,
Each breath a bell,
Each exhale a prayer remembered by the body.

We are temples of silence and song.
The ribs are arches, the spine a column,
And through the open door of the mouth
The spirit enters, radiant and unafraid.

Even in sorrow, breath kneels inside us.
Even in grief, it lifts its hymn.
It says: Rise, though your knees remember dust.
It says: Sing, though your voice has forgotten.
It says: Live, though the grave has already whispered your name.

The cathedral of breath has no steeple,
No stone but the body enduring.
It stands wherever a soul leans toward light.
And there, the choir is endless.

The Monarch

She rose from a stone still damp with dew,
Her wings thin as silence,
Yet the air parted for her
As though it knew her name.

The oak, ancient and rooted,
Watched her pass without protest.
She carried no burden
But the memory of distances,
The invisible map of survival
Written in her flight.

I thought then:
Power does not always thunder.
Sometimes it drifts,
Gold and fragile,
Across a field of ordinary light.

And in her going,
She blessed the morning—
Reminding me
That even what seems delicate
Can outlast storms,
And even what is small
Can lead us forward.

The Ocean Inside Us

Inside me the ocean moves,
Its salt stinging my veins,
Its waves breaking against the ribs
That cannot contain it.

The sea is older than memory,
Older than the scars of earth,
Older than the silence of stone.

And still it speaks
In gulls circling,
In thunder rolled across water,
In the nets of fishermen
Who wake before dawn.

Do not tell me we are small.
The ocean lives within us,
A tide that will not surrender,
A blue fire folding its weight
Into our every breath.

When the last shore crumbles,
It will rise again in us,
Endless,
Without fear,
A body of water walking upright
Into the future

Morning Stillness

The morning is still.
No clock strikes.
The pond holds the sky
Without ripple or question.

I listen,
And the silence
Is not empty
It is full,
Like a hand extended,
Like light resting on stone.

The day begins
Without demand.
I walk into it,
Lighter than before,
Carrying nothing
But breath.

www.ingramcontent.com/pod-product-compliance
Lightning Source LLC
Chambersburg PA
CBHW012023050526
44107CB00102B/717